THE TALE OF PETER RABBIT

Coloring Book

Based on the original story by
Beatrix Potter

Ideals Children's Books • Nashville, Tennessee

Copyright © 1996 by Hambleton-Hill Publishing, Inc.
All rights reserved.
Published by Ideals Children's Books
An imprint of Hambleton-Hill Publishing, Inc.
Nashville, Tennessee 37218
Printed and bound in the United States of America

ISBN 1-57102-068-3

Once upon a time there were four little Rabbits, and their names were Flopsy, Mopsy, Cotton-tail, and Peter.

They lived with their mother in a sand-bank,
underneath the root of a very big fir-tree.

"Now, my dears," said Mrs. Rabbit one morning, "you may go into the fields or down the lane, but don't go into Mr. McGregor's garden. Now run along, and don't get into mischief. I am going out."

But Peter, who was very naughty, ran straight away to Mr. McGregor's garden, and squeezed under the gate!

First he ate some lettuces and French beans; and
then he ate some radishes. Then, feeling rather sick, he
went to look for some parsley.

But round the end of a cucumber frame was Mr. McGregor! He jumped up and ran after Peter, calling out, "Stop thief!"

Peter rushed all over the garden, but he had forgotten
the way back to the gate. He lost one of his shoes among
the cabbages, and the other shoe amongst the potatoes.

He might have gotten away if he had not run into a gooseberry net, and got caught by the buttons on his jacket. It was a blue jacket with brass buttons, quite new.

Peter gave himself up for lost. His sobs were overheard by some sparrows who implored him to exert himself. Peter wriggled out just in time, leaving his jacket behind him.

Peter rushed into the tool-shed, and jumped into a can.
It would have been a beautiful thing to hide in if it had
not had so much water in it.

Mr. McGregor was quite sure that Peter was in the tool-shed, perhaps hidden underneath a flower-pot. He began to turn each one over carefully.

Presently Peter sneezed—"Kertyschoo!" Mr.
McGregor was after him in no time, but Peter jumped
out of a window, upsetting three plants.

Peter sat down outside to rest; he was out of breath, trembling with fright, and he had no idea which way to go. Also he was very damp.

After a time, he began to wander about, going
lippity-lippity—not very fast, and looking all around.

An old mouse was running in and out over a stone
doorstep. Peter asked her the way to the gate, but she
had a pea in her mouth and could not answer.

Presently, he came to a pond. A white cat was staring at some goldfish. Peter thought it best to go away without speaking to her; he had heard about cats from his cousin, Benjamin Bunny.

Peter went back towards the tool-shed, but suddenly, quite close to him, he heard the noise of a hoe—sc-r-ritch, scratch, scratch, scritch.

It was Mr. McGregor hoeing onions, and beyond him was the gate.

Peter started running as fast as he could go. Mr. McGregor caught sight of him, but Peter slipped underneath the gate, and was safe at last in the wood outside the garden.

Mr. McGregor hung up the little jacket and the shoes
for a scarecrow to frighten the blackbirds.

Peter never stopped running or looked behind him
till he got home to the big fir-tree.

I am sorry to say that Peter was not very well during the evening. His mother put him to bed, and made some camomile tea. And she gave a dose of it to Peter!

But Flopsy, Mopsy, and Cotton-tail had bread and milk and blackberries for supper.

The End